Stop Smoking

The Definitive Manual For Achieving Permanent
Smoking Cessation Without Enduring Mental Stress

*(Effective Strategies And Holistic Methods For Achieving
Permanent Smoking Cessation)*

Sebastien Daniels

TABLE OF CONTENT

The Temptation Of My Base Instincts And Surrendering Command.. 1

The Influence Of Hope 8

Developing An Effective Strategy For Smoking Cessation 21

Link Up With Your Goal...54

What Are The Reasons To Cease Smoking? 76

Nicotine Replacement Therapy (Nrt) As A Means Of Providing Physical Assistance In Smoking Cessation 111

Therapeutic Herbal Remedies For Smoking Cessation 118

The Temptation Of My Base Instincts And Surrendering Command

The severity of my tobacco dependency reached such an extent that in the absence of cigarettes, I exhibited irritable behavior towards my spouse and offspring. This habit was exceedingly detrimental. I am sincerely grateful for the continued presence of my family, as I am fully aware that I am undeserving of their support. My wife was very loyal to me amidst of all that drama, even though I treated her horribly. She remained steadfastly by my side and exerted every effort within her capabilities to aid me. She is undeniably a celestial being dispatched by the divine force. I have solemnly vowed to uphold, cherish, and prioritize the well-being of my wife for the entirety of my lifetime. I am thoroughly impressed by her exceptional abilities.

It is widely recognized that cigarette smoking has a detrimental impact on one's health, particularly the nervous system. Therefore, what are the reasons behind the persistent tobacco consumption among individuals? There is a belief held by certain individuals that smokers exhibit a lack of concern towards their own well-being. After having grappled with this affliction for a span of just over seventeen years, I respectfully beg to differ! It is my firm conviction that the majority of individuals who partake in the act of smoking tobacco possess a genuine desire to relinquish this habit, albeit often unaware of their own potential to do so. It represents a substantive struggle that the majority of individuals fail to grasp, and are generally unaware of the profound difficulty that goes into its cessation. In an earnest endeavor, I strive to provide support and inspiration to individuals grappling with addiction, by openly recounting my personal journey. The adverse impact on the human body is widely recognized, therefore, rather than reiterating what is already known to most smokers, I choose to relate my personal encounters to them. I am confident that anyone can quit smoking, even after an extended period such as seventeen years. I empathize with the profound frustration and distress experienced by individuals who are addicted to cigarettes. I made numerous attempts to quit, all of which ended in failure; however, this did not deter me from persistently striving to quit. There was a period during which I achieved success in abstaining from nicotine, leading to one month of complete freedom from it. I experienced immense satisfaction in realizing that I possessed the fortitude and bravery to relinquish it. Upon encountering turmoil upon my threshold, I resorted to partaking in the act of smoking once more.

The Lesson
Don't Give Up
After enduring numerous challenges and hardships, I acquired an understanding of the soothing nature of nicotine, particularly during moments of turmoil. Based on observable evidence, it is

evident that you are not the only one in this situation. Persevere even though you have made multiple attempts without success. It is completely commonplace, as everyone experiences this. It is a procedural undertaking that necessitates a substantial investment of time and patience. As the duration of nicotine abstinence increases, the level of dependence on it progressively diminishes within the human body. The crucial factor lies in perseverance. Despite the challenges that may appear insurmountable, strive to cultivate a stress-free environment. Attempting to cease the habit of smoking in a time of heightened stress can prove to be a formidable task. That will merely contribute to the stimulation of the desire for further nicotine consumption.

During my second attempt, I successfully refrained from smoking for a notable duration of three months. Consequently, I experienced a substantial increase in my energy levels, consistently waking up to a refreshing breath every morning, and significantly reduced instances of daytime lethargy without any apparent cause. Subsequently, I was contacted by my father, an occurrence that had a profound impact on the course of my existence.

He addressed me, saying, "Son, I regret to inform you that I have received unfortunate news."

I asked, "What?"

He stated, "The caller identifies himself as your Uncle Claudio."

May I inquire about the current status of Claudio?

"He died. Someone murdered him".

I found it incredulous to comprehend the auditory information that was being conveyed to me. Was this a joke? Was I being punked? I entertained the notion that my father might be engaging in a distasteful jest, given his propensity for humor. However, on this occasion, it was authentic. I instantaneously experienced trembling, tears, and vocal outbursts. Why? What happened? Who did it? I experienced profound anger and bewilderment. My sole preoccupation was seeking retribution. My initial action involved proceeding to the nearest establishment and acquiring a package of Newport 100's. I consecutively consumed approximately five cigarettes. Subsequently, I found myself ensnared once more. I was aware that my actions of resuming smoking were incorrect. I was already aware of this fact. It was merely a single pack. It is not a significant matter. However, subsequently, I found myself engaged in a struggle against this entity known as nicotine once more. I indulged in smoking continuously, and before I knew it, an entire decade had elapsed. This is the period during which I frequently engaged in chain smoking. One pack after another. It is an indispensable component of my life. I engaged in smoking immediately upon awakening, prior to consuming meals, subsequent to consuming meals, preceding sexual activity, following sexual activity, and at every feasible opportunity. I was strongly inclined towards resignation and remained aware that this distressing situation would eventually draw to a close. I persisted resolutely, unwavering in my determination and refusal to surrender. That is the reason I am presently capable of penning this book in order to convey my personal narrative to you and to inspire you to cease your actions. As previously mentioned, if it is within my ability to cease this activity, it is also within yours.

The Influence Of Hope

There exists a considerable disparity between the experience of being in the company of an optimistic individual versus that of being in the presence of a pessimistic individual. The positive person attracts a lot of positive people inside his circle while the negative person draws them away. You typically wouldn't choose to accompany an individual with a negative disposition, correct? This phenomenon occurs due to the tendency of negativity to attract negativity. An individual displaying a positive disposition frequently exhibits a cheerful countenance, experiences a heightened sense of contentment and gratitude towards numerous aspects, thereby rendering their company enjoyable. Typically, he garners more popularity, achievement, and respect within the community, educational environment, and even his own household. The individual possessing a positive demeanor is held in higher regard and receives greater affection from those around them. Conversely, individuals with a negative outlook are frequently isolated, shunned by others, and subjected to mistreatment or harassment. Their pessimistic perspective on life leads to their experience of misfortunes and adversities. Indeed, the efficacy of thoughts is truly remarkable. It possesses the propensity to draw towards oneself whatever thoughts are harbored, whether they bear negative or positive connotations...

What impact can a positive mindset have on an individual?

1. Positive thinking can greatly enhance one's capabilities and unlock a multitude

of opportunities. A study conducted by psychologists revealed that adopting a positive mindset has the potential to broaden good prospects and amplify inherent abilities in individuals. They assigned five groups the task of observing video clips. Two cohorts were assigned to view video clips depicting positive emotions such as contentment and happiness. One group observed a video containing emotions that were carefully balanced, while the other two groups viewed videos expressing feelings of anger and disappointment. Upon observing, they were instructed to articulate the actions they intend to undertake. Psychologists have determined that individuals who viewed the positive video clips exhibited a higher propensity for written productivity compared to those exposed to negative and neutral stimuli. This means that positive thoughts pave the way to more possibilities for the person to enhance creative thinking skills and apply it on their daily life.

2. Positive emotions yield long-term advantages: When a child is brought up in a positive milieu, their prospects for positive growth are significantly enhanced. If he is stimulated with optimistic sentiments such as delight, amusement, inventiveness, companionship, amusement, and affection, a constructive mindset arises and this optimistic outlook endures as he develops and pursues his aspirations in life. Despite the waning of positive emotions, the enduring repercussions it imparts upon the individual persist over the long haul, bearing potential utility spanning the entirety of their lifetime. Conversely, in the event that a child is raised in a setting that necessitates the suppression of their natural inclinations and subjects them to conditions

embodying hatred, deprivation, adversity, illness, abandonment, and harm, it is highly probable that said child will develop distorted perspectives regarding existence. It is highly probable that his life will exhibit tendencies of both insignificance and defiance. The adverse emotions that he experienced in his youth were a magnet for undesirable and unfortunate circumstances.

3. Optimism contributes to and fosters a sense of happiness: Individuals who possess happiness exhibit a positive outlook, and those with a positive disposition tend to experience happiness. It is impossible for it to be otherwise.

PREVIOUSLY ACQUIRED KNOWLEDGE REGARDING CIGARETTES

The aspect that greatly troubles me regarding smoking is not the diseases that are commonly associated with it, but rather the recurring nature of the habit—persistent and repeated instances of smoking on an hourly, daily, monthly, and yearly basis, exerting strain on the respiratory system and other crucial bodily organs. As the commonly held belief suggests, any experience that does not result in fatality has the potential to contribute to personal growth and improvement. However, it is evident to all that these particular circumstances have lethal consequences. However, despite this fact, we all persist in smoking as a result of our brain being deceived by this addictive habit. It fostered the belief within us that these cigarettes are necessary for social interaction during activities such as drinking coffee, after meals, and other customary cigarette-associated rituals.

Upon commencing my enrollment in the University with the intention of pursuing a degree in Engineering, I had not anticipated regressing into the pernicious habit of tobacco consumption. I have demonstrated my ability to endure without such dependencies, and I was unaware that the allure of this habit would ensnare me—I was caught off guard. I have abstained from smoking for a duration of four years. However, I recently observed its recurrence, attributing it to a triggering sensation that I experienced during that time. I experienced fatigue and unease, leading me to deem a cigarette necessary.

I hold a strong conviction that our cognitive faculties have been conditioned by this phenomenon to persist in smoking and escalate our consumption of cigarettes. It is imperative to consider the gravity of this addiction and acknowledge the detrimental impact it has on both our physical well-being and the broader fabric of our society, and potentially even on civilization itself.

What course of action should we pursue? One of the strategies I employ after smoking is referred to as the chain reaction technique. This involves subtly influencing individuals in your vicinity to engage in similar behaviors and responses. Once you abstain from smoking, you, as an individual, possess the ability and determination to influence those in your vicinity to discontinue the habit. Potential sources of value might include your colleagues, family members, spouse, and other individuals.

You have the capability to undertake this commitment as a former smoker and take an oath to assist others in quitting. It would be a task easily accomplished as long as you embrace a smoke-free lifestyle and show determination to succeed.

The undisclosed narrative behind the reliance on cigarettes

Over the course of recent decades, our collective understanding of the adverse health effects of smoking has become well-established. Smoking has been linked to a range of debilitating conditions including but not limited to lung and heart diseases, as well as ailments affecting the throat and gums. Nevertheless, the information regarding the cigarettes has not been adequately documented and remains undisclosed to the public. These factors have multifaceted detrimental effects on us— not limited to smoking-related illnesses, but rather pertaining to the behavioral influence exerted by cigarettes.

Allow me to elaborate; these factors educate, mislead, and manipulate us into developing a dependency on smoking. We remain largely unaware of this phenomenon due to the widespread legality associated with the purchase of such items from nearly any location. Smoking harbors a clandestine virtue - its inherent intelligence surpasses our own, as evidenced by our compulsion to partake in its consumption in spite of our superior intellect. Smoking is permissible, and while it may not inherently be deemed improper, our persistent indulgence in this habit can be attributed to being ensnared by its allure. The crucial aspect of quitting lies in breaking free from this enthrallment and exercising greater wisdom over one's engagement with cigarettes.

One strategy I employed to quit smoking was through the use of ingenuity; I developed a heightened level of cleverness to outsmart my addiction. I dedicated considerable time to studying my addiction, accumulating extensive knowledge about its nature over the course of several years. Additionally, I wish to avoid succumbing to her influence—and I trust the same applies to you.

Developing An Effective Strategy For Smoking Cessation

Having comprehended the advantages that can be derived from abstaining from tobacco smoking, you might possibly be inclined to cease this habit; nonetheless, you might currently be uncertain about the initial steps to undertake. Let us now examine the process of formulating a comprehensive strategy for smoking cessation.

Set a Quit Date

Take a firm stance against smoking by establishing a committed quit date. When selecting the date, please bear in mind that it should be scheduled during a time when you are experiencing minimal stress. It could occur on a momentous occasion such as a birthday, or on any other day, as long as you abide by it. Aligning the date at which you plan to quit smoking with any personal objectives you have established would be optimal. For example, certain individuals on this occasion may opt to cease smoking entirely, while others will strive to decrease their intake of cigarettes to a specific threshold. Regardless of the circumstances, it is imperative that you demonstrate reverence and uphold the importance of that specified date.

Prepare Yourself

Arriving at the determination to cease smoking is a formidable task, and the subsequent adherence to such a decision is even more arduous. Prioritize equipping yourself with an understanding of the anticipated circumstances to proactively mitigate potential disillusionments during the ensuing process. The initial point to grasp is that discontinuing smoking is a rather challenging endeavor, necessitating readiness for potential setbacks. Develop a comprehensive support strategy to effectively address and manage moments of intense desire, along with a corresponding incentive framework that effectively maintains your motivation and commitment towards achieving your objectives. It is imperative that you thoroughly eradicate any traces of smoking from your residence and diligently sanitize all areas to eradicate all manifestations of smoking. In order to achieve optimal outcomes, it is advisable to eliminate all triggering factors and implement a comprehensive transformation in your lifestyle.

Support

Engaging in smoking is a demanding endeavor. Nicotine possesses a strong propensity for addiction and the accompanying withdrawal symptoms prompt an almost immediate desire to engage in smoking shortly after cessation. Nevertheless, it is crucial to establish a system of support when faced with the onset of cravings and compulsions. The intended objective of the requisite assistance is to minimize or completely redirect your attention away from smoking while reinforcing the significance of this matter. You have the option to seek assistance from your physician who can prescribe medication and recommend supplementary products designed to alleviate cravings. Support helplines are typically staffed by individuals who have quit smoking themselves, thereby rendering them a valuable source of assistance. Furthermore, one's own family and friends inherently serve as the most organic support network. Nowadays, one can readily access smartphone applications that aid in maintaining accountability and facilitating progress throughout this journey.

Instances of relapse are to be expected, so it is advised to be adequately prepared.

It is essential to remain vigilant at all times, as at any given moment, you might succumb to your desires. Relapses are a common occurrence, evidenced by statistical data indicating that the majority of smokers undergo approximately 5 to 7 attempts before achieving permanent cessation of cigarette use. Do not allow yourself to become disillusioned and overwhelmed by a relapse, to the extent that you return to your previous habit. Instead, perceive each setback as a valuable learning opportunity and utilize these challenges as catalysts for personal growth. Resume your pursuit with the newfound experience and steadfastly strive towards the achievement of your goals, regardless of the gradual pace at which progress may be made.

Find Motivation

It is essential for you to seek out sources of inspiration. If you have acquired this book, it signifies your inclination to embark upon the journey of quitting smoking. Congratulate yourself for this. Presently, what is the reason for your decision to discontinue smoking? In the end, the decision must be based on what is in your best interest. Otherwise, you will encounter significant challenges in mustering the motivation to cease. Therefore, it is conceivable that your motivation stems from both concerns regarding your well-being as well as considerations regarding the impressions and evaluations made by others in relation to your smoking habit. It would be advisable to engage in the preliminary exercise of creating a pie chart (accuracy is not essential) that effectively depicts the varying degrees of importance assigned to different motivations for quitting smoking.

I shall address the topic of setting goals in due course, once we have acquired additional information upon which to conceive our objectives.

Secondary Motivation Task: Elaborate at length on the factors that inspire and drive you. In an alternative approach, it is advisable to communicate with a child or an individual whom you hold deep concern for, expressing the reasons as to why they should refrain from smoking. Subsequently, it would be prudent to reflect upon those very recommendations and apply them to yourself, considering that they are equally applicable.

Addictive qualities

You may be familiar with the substance known as Nicotine and its detrimental effects on health, as well as its highly addictive nature. You may have disregarded these assertions in order to justify a smoking habit, and you would not be in the minority in doing so. Nicotine can be detected in tobacco, the substance commonly consumed through smoking cigarettes. It possesses a level of addictiveness that surpasses that of illicit substances such as heroin or cocaine. Owing to its impact on the chemistry of the brain, individuals may experience unpleasant withdrawal symptoms, analogous to the effects associated with substances such as cocaine and heroin. Essentially, upon smoking, the brain becomes exposed to nicotine, resulting in the development of additional nicotine receptors and a subsequent craving for more. Consequently, when one decides to cease smoking, negative side effects are likely to occur. However, it remains advantageous in the long run.

Cigarettes may not appear to be as perilous as illicit substances, yet they inflict severe adverse consequences with the potential to jeopardize one's life. There exist additional substances and chemicals in numerous cigarettes that exacerbate the challenge of cessation. However, the comprehensive investigation of these chemicals and their associated impacts by medical professionals and researchers is still lacking.

Reasons people smoke?

The underlying factors contributing to an individual's smoking habit extend beyond mere dependency on the chemicals present in tobacco products. It ultimately boils down to an emotional reliance as well.

1) The presence of physical and chemical reliance leading to addiction

2) Smoking, in and of itself, cultivates a habitual and comforting behavior.

3) To alleviate or alleviate feelings of stress, anger, anxiety, fear, and depression – alongside other emotions or circumstances that may incite the inclination.

There exist notable parallels among dependencies on drugs, alcohol, self-harm, and smoking, as they all inevitably lead to addiction. We commence or persist prior to becoming chemically dependent, as we are attempting to address a deficiency or engage in self-medication to some extent. The issue at hand is that it functions effectively. Temporarily. We experience a sense of tranquility when we engage in smoking as a means of coping with a conflictual interaction with our employer. However, this approach is not conducive to promoting overall well-being, as it poses risks to both physical and emotional health.

It is imperative to take personal responsibility, and at times, seeking the assistance of a trusted friend or family member is essential in achieving this objective. Occasionally, it proves beneficial for friends to collectively engage in quiet contemplation and mutually uplift one another. Occasionally, it can be advantageous to request a friend or family member to refrain from providing you with something in the event of a setback, or alternatively, regularly inquire about your progress. It would be beneficial to consider maintaining a public record of your progress by utilizing a platform such as Facebook or another suitable medium. In addition to providing you with accountability, they will also offer you encouragement and support.

Assignment on Personal Accountability: Inform one or more individuals of your endeavor to discontinue the mentioned activity. Compose an electronic mail, transmit a text message, initiate a telephone conversation—convey your objective and earnestly solicit their backing.

Adverse consequences of tobacco cessation.

The adverse effects of cessation can be quite challenging due to the presence of a nicotine dependency that is intricately linked to cerebral activity, consequently impacting one's physiological well-being. You have developed a physiological dependence in your brain, alongside an accompanying psychological attachment. Symptoms will include:

• Strong urges or the inclination to engage in smoking

• Oscillations in emotional state • Fluctuations in mood • Variations in emotional disposition • Swings in emotional temperament

• Fatigue

• Overall physical unease

• Constipation

- Symptoms resembling those of influenza
- Increase in body weight • Accumulation of excess pounds • Growth in overall mass • Augmentation of body size through increased weight

SECTION 2

How to quit smoking

You may be pondering the question, "How can one effectively cease the habit of smoking?" Indeed, it is an undeniable reality that there exists no effortless method of cessation, nor any mystical, expeditious approach to break free from this habitual behavior. In my experience, the most effective approach entails gradually discontinuing their use. The abrupt cessation approach, known as "Cold Turkey," can yield favorable outcomes for certain individuals, albeit it may pose significant discomfort and risks for others. If you typically consume ten cigarettes per day, reduce your intake to nine cigarettes the following day. It won't be easy. Gradually discontinue your reliance on them, while ensuring that you maintain a sense of responsibility and determination. The intended purpose of this book is to provide assistance in fostering motivation and accountability.

Setting goals

Goal setting is difficult. But the best way I've found to hold yourself accountable is to make little goals and create a reward system to encourage yourself. Your ultimate objective could be to cease smoking permanently. However, in order to achieve your ultimate objective, it is imperative to establish intermediate milestones. It is essential to further break down each of these milestones into even smaller objectives, to ensure successful completion, no matter how minute they may seem. Each accomplishment should be regarded as a cause for celebration, regardless of its apparent insignificance.

Objective Task: Compile a comprehensive list of goals pertaining to cessation of smoking, followed by the formulation of subordinate goals beneath each one, progressively breaking them down to a manageable level.

A potential hindrance to individuals attempting to undertake a task is their apprehension of failure. Reconceptualize your notion of failure, and perceive errors as occasions for growth and advancement. Furthermore, do not allow apprehension of a potential relapse to hinder your determination in seeking to cease smoking.

Addressing Concerns of Relapse: Compose a formal correspondence to provide oneself solace and encouragement akin to consoling a trusted companion following a setback, emphasizing the importance of perseverance and discouraging surrender. Do not allow apprehension of a potential regression impede your efforts in abstaining.

Compose a formal letter addressed to your own self, commencing with the salutation "Dear ___, in the event that you are perusing this correspondence, it denotes that you have experienced a relapse in your endeavors. However, it is essential to acknowledge that this circumstance is acceptable and should not be a cause for distress." Currently, I am situated in this position, engaged in the act of composing this correspondence, and I am experiencing a state of contentment. I have successfully abstained from reverting to my past behavior for ___ consecutive days, and I would like to inform you that despite your relapse, your diligent efforts have greatly contributed to my current progress. And it is not yet appropriate to desist from making efforts.

Now, I would like to task you with another related assignment, wherein I request your response or answer to the given query, simulating a conversational context. Allow me to elucidate: Imagine a scenario where I am positioned as your confidant, who is striving to overcome the habit of smoking, while you provide the necessary motivation to prevent me from abandoning my objective. The objective of this assignment is to demonstrate that we exhibit greater levels of compassion and rationality towards others, extending more forgiveness towards their errors, in comparison to the expectations we hold for ourselves. If we were to envision our companion encountering the identical circumstances that we presently face, and contemplate the guidance we would offer them, it begets the question: why not extend the same counsel to ourselves? Do not become your own adversary through the habit of smoking, or at any time.

Please find enclosed the Conversation Assignment: "

Me: I relapsed. I'm such a failure.

You:

I: However, I did engage in smoking despite my previous declaration of abstaining from it. I have nullified all the effort I invested in achieving a period of __ consecutive days without smoking, rendering it devoid of any value.

You:

Me: What course of action should I take now? May I resume smoking, given that I have made a mistake?

You:

Now I would like to draw your attention to the fact that the points you expressed in response to me (your acquaintance) hold equal merit and relevance to both yourself and your friend. These are the utterances that you ought to be directing towards yourself. Be your own friend.

Adverse Effects of Smoking on Human Health.

Addiction

The condition of addiction, or more precisely, the state of dependence, constitutes a significant health repercussion that is prevalent across various forms of tobacco consumption. Although addiction alone does not lead to fatality, it does contribute significantly to the detrimental health consequences associated with smoking, as it reinforces consistent consumption of an extremely toxic substance.

Cigarettes exhibit a high propensity for addiction due to the administration of substantial levels of nicotine into the lungs, which is swiftly transported via the bloodstream to the brain. Notwithstanding the abundant historical records indicating the transformation of smoking into an addiction for certain individuals who indulge in it.

Nicotine, in its entirety, induces addictive tendencies and instigates physiological ramifications. The activation of reward circuits within the brain gives rise to behavioral outcomes and physiological cravings, resulting in prolonged usage, tolerance, and physical reliance, along with the manifestation of withdrawal symptoms upon abrupt cessation. Nicotine alone is not the sole factor in tobacco that contributes to addiction. Many individuals derive significant pleasure from the various chemicals present in tobacco smoke, particularly those that elicit sensory stimulation.

The flavors and aromas of cigarettes can be intensified by incorporating substances such as ammonia, menthol, levulinic acid, and even chocolate.

Cigarettes exhibit a higher degree of addictiveness in comparison to alternative nicotine replacement therapies, such as patches and gum, owing to nicotine's pronounced sensory and other impacts. (Refer below to the section under "Quitting Smoking.")

When an individual inhales a deep breath of nicotine-containing smoke, the nicotine is promptly absorbed by the lungs and transported into the bloodstream simultaneously with the oxygen. In less than a span of 10 seconds, nicotine swiftly traverses from the respiratory system to the cerebral region upon inhalation. The mechanism of action of nicotine involves its binding to specific receptor proteins located on the surfaces of neurons within the central and peripheral nervous systems.

Upon the attachment of a nicotine particle to a nicotine receptor on a neuron, the transmission of nerve impulses is initiated. The physiological and behavioral repercussions of nicotine emerge as a consequence of this mechanism, which facilitates the transmission of neurotransmitters, or chemical signaling molecules.

For example, nicotine induces a rise in blood pressure and heart rate, boosts alertness and concentration by provoking the secretion of adrenaline and norepinephrine through the stimulation of the adrenal glands. The release of the neurotransmitter dopamine is also observed as a result of the stimulation caused by nicotine. Certain researchers posit that dopamine is of paramount importance in nicotine's reinforcement and gratifying impact on the emotional state.

The vast majority of smokers have had negative early experiences with lighting up. Novice smokers occasionally experience dizziness, nausea, and emesis as a result of the nicotine content within tobacco products. Through repeated practice, individuals who smoke gain the ability to ascertain the precise amount of nicotine necessary to accomplish their desired outcomes.

Nevertheless, as the consumption of nicotine escalates, the physiological response entails an augmented production of nicotine receptors. This phenomenon is referred to as nicotine tolerance, and it results in the smoker requiring progressively higher quantities of nicotine in order to achieve the identical outcome. Once an individual's body has developed resistance to nicotine and continued to consume it in elevated quantities, a state of physiological dependence ensues. Consequently, if one abruptly stops smoking without any gradual reduction, withdrawal symptoms can arise.

These encompass symptoms such as memory lapse, moodiness, increase in body weight, feelings of sadness, unease, inability to sleep, and persistent urges for food. In the span of one week, the symptoms are expected to peak before gradually subsiding. However, it is important to note that experiences may vary among individuals, as certain individuals may develop enduring cravings that persist for an extended period of time.

Nicotine's impact on mood modulation, appetite regulation, cognitive concentration, and focus are plausible elements that potentially contribute to the sustained efficacy of tobacco consumption in the long run. The phenomenon of physical dependence contributes to a variety of these results.

As an example, extended utilization of nicotine can foster a heightened physiological reliance and exacerbate the adverse effects experienced during the cessation process.

A temporary solution to alleviate the discomfort caused by withdrawal is to recommence the act of smoking. The individual who smokes might erroneously infer that smoking enhances mood and boosts performance due to the temporary alleviation of withdrawal symptoms caused by nicotine cessation. However, this assumption is unfounded.

From the perspective of smokers, this can exert a substantial influence. Cigarette smokers frequently exhibit lower body weight than non-smokers, typically ranging between 2 to 4 kg (4.4 to 8.8 pounds), and weight gain is often observed upon smoking cessation.

Weight that has been gained may potentially be reduced through the assistance of a resumption of smoking. Similarly, individuals may find themselves unable to perform their duties or engage in academic and extracurricular pursuits due to nicotine withdrawal, sometimes encompassing only a few hours. The habitual smoker may become cognizant of the fact that even a single pack of cigarettes exerts a substantial impact on their capacity to concentrate and accomplish assignments.

The addictive properties of nicotine are present in all widely known tobacco brands. Nevertheless, diverse tobacco products exhibit distinct addictive usage patterns that are contingent upon a multitude of circumstances. Increasing the price of tobacco products and restricting access to them has been shown to reduce tobacco usage (and hence the usage of drugs) and even encourage some smokers to give up the habit altogether.

The usage of cigars and pipes is typically observed at a significantly later stage compared to cigarettes among the majority of individuals, and it is common for those who do adopt this practice to inhale lower quantities of the tobacco vapor. While it is undeniable that a significant number of individuals who indulge in cigar and pipe smoking do develop a strong dependency, the overall prevalence of addiction appears to be lower when compared to the prevalence rate observed for cigarette consumption.

When nicotine is rapidly absorbed into the body, it elicits its distinct pleasurable psychoactive effects; however, this concomitantly elevates the susceptibility to developing addiction. Despite the fact that the delivery of nicotine through snuff and chewing tobacco is slower compared to inhaling cigarette smoke, numerous individuals find its convenient and effortless utilization to be captivating and ultimately habit-forming.

Link Up With Your Goal

No individual refrains from smoking cessation without a compelling rationale.

I am inclined to share a comprehensive account of my entire journey throughout my "smoking career," as I aspire to expose myself to vulnerability. It commenced at the age of fifteen with the initial cigarette and ultimately concluded in my early thirties with my final interaction with tobacco. Contrary to the majority who quit, I am unable to provide you with a specific date. It is not recorded in my schedule. All I know is it was a Sunday in August, three to four years ago.

Throughout the period in which I engaged in smoking, there were intermittent intervals of indulgence and abstinence, with the habit of heavy smoking not firmly established until my late twenties. During that period, one of the factors that contributed to my smoking habit was the observation that many attractive females were engaged in the act of smoking. I found that frequenting the designated smoking area adjacent to a bar or club, wherein individuals were compelled to assemble, greatly facilitated the initiation of dialogues.

Initially, I would casually carry a lighter in my pocket and socialize, but subsequently, I transformed into the individual who consistently possessed a package of cigarettes. My addiction spiraled out of control. Subsequent to abstaining from frequenting bars and clubs and no longer seeking to establish new acquaintances, subsequent to entering into matrimony and commencing parenthood, I persistently indulged in smoking, despite the absence of its original motivation.

I started smoking as I believed it enhanced my appearance. Throughout the period when I was a smoker, I made numerous attempts to cease the habit for various reasons. However, one significant obstacle that impeded my progress was the persistent influence of those around me who would consistently tempt me with cigarettes, often suggesting that I postpone my cessation efforts. It would be prudent to only have a single one, as it is not of great consequence."

I did not encounter significant peer pressure, however, I observed that when one chooses to cease smoking, their companions who engage in smoking begin to experience a sense of solitude. You serve as a reflection of their poor decision-making, and by preventing you from resigning, they can mitigate the intensification of their guilt.

What is the rationale behind your decision?

There reaches a juncture wherein one declares, "I shall no longer tolerate this." I must effect a modification. Until you solidify your alignment with the appropriate purpose for yourself, it will prove exceedingly difficult to sever this habitual pattern.

My attempts at discontinuing the habit of smoking proved to be futile, as I was motivated by both the alarming demise of my uncle and concerns regarding potential long-term health complications. Every pack of cigarettes in the world has a warning or a picture on it of someone dying from smoking, and yet people still smoke from those packs all the time. The long-term alert is ineffective.

One aspect that we will emphasize in this book pertains to the cultivation of wholesome habits that align with your fundamental motivation, the precise rationale behind your desire to cease smoking.

The fundamental reason that motivated me, as I gazed into my daughter's eyes during that instance, was the aspiration to be by her side, to provide support, and to become a more exemplary paternal figure. That evolved into my fundamental principle. On each occasion that I endeavored to renounce my habit for the sake of my spouse, motivated by the desire to provide her with an improved existence and spare her from the unpleasantness of being in close proximity to someone with an offensive odor, my efforts proved ineffectual.

What is the central purpose or motivation behind your actions?

When delineating the cause for your desire to cease, it becomes crucial to ascertain your aspirations in life. Given the limited amount of time available to you each day, it is prudent to prioritize the tasks that yield the most significant impact or return on investment. It pertains to a straightforward procedure of discerning your genuine priorities and constructing a regimen that facilitates the sustenance of your livelihood.

We have thoroughly examined extensive lists of advantages and extensively discussed every aspect of your life. The primary objective behind undertaking this initial step was to simplify your response to this question. It is advised that you select a fundamental objective that aligns most strongly with your personal values and aspirations. It is not necessary for it to be identical to mine. Perhaps, one of your primary motivations stems from a desire to restore the cleanliness and aesthetic quality of your teeth. Embrace the reason that strikes a chord with you and firmly hold onto it.

Ideally, it would be advisable to select a primary objective that aligns with being of shorter duration. Short-term objectives wield greater influence. When a distant objective is identified, individuals face difficulties in their endeavor to attain it while also attempting to envisage it. Only a small minority of individuals possess the ability to devise a strategic approach that spans fifteen years and remain steadfast in their pursuit.

When one fixates on a distant objective, it can prove exceptionally challenging to remain steadfast, as one must contend with daily impulses. Initially, this pertains to adhering to a routine that can be promptly undertaken. During the initial weeks and months of cessation, abstaining from smoking necessitated a daily undertaking. If you have participated in any of the anonymous programs such as Alcoholics Anonymous or Narcotics Anonymous, you would likely be familiar with their overarching approach of embracing the concept of "living in the present moment" as the foundation of their methodology.

Our objective is to prioritize the pursuit of daily victories. Upon achieving victory for seven consecutive days, one may ascertain the successful culmination of a week. Upon achieving a consecutive winning streak of thirty days, you have emerged victorious for an entire month. We are in the process of establishing the aforementioned methodology, which commences with the presence of a goal sufficiently proximate to instill motivation for conquering daily challenges.

Instances of Fundamental Reasons to Utilize

There exists a multitude of exemplary instances of fundamental objectives at your disposal. The primary concern is the occurrence of sickness or the anxiety surrounding it. I experienced an array of respiratory ailments and difficulties breathing, yet it did not prove sufficient to prompt me to cease. However, the prospect of grappling with emphysema or the necessity of sleeping with a respiratory mask or an oxygen apparatus could be the focal point of your concerns.

Arguably, health can be considered the most compelling rationale in your case. You desire increased swiftness, the ability to resume running, reclaim your youthful vigor, and regain the capacity to execute exercises such as jumping jacks or actively participate in dodgeball once more. The yearning to engage in the sports of one's earlier years or take part in activities previously unfulfilled can engender a sense of dedication and serve as a driving force.

Family can serve as an additional compelling factor. Perhaps you have experienced the loss of a family member, desire to establish a connection with another individual, or aspire to serve as a positive influence in someone's life.

Fear works well too. If one harbors concerns regarding mortality or illness, such thoughts can serve as a compelling impetus. Fear exhibits immense potency as an emotion, and upon experiencing instances of temptation, one shall discern that fear surpasses desire in strength. It will facilitate your successful progress and maintain your perseverance.

Ultimately, stress could be the fundamental reason behind your current predicament. Cigarette consumption engenders a state of psychological tension, where this tension represents a manifestation of chronic or protracted daily apprehension. If one constantly dwells upon the notion of quitting smoking, experiencing escalating stress due to feeling trapped in a repetitive pattern, then the concept of alleviating such stress and reducing blood pressure may occupy one's thoughts on a daily basis.

I would recommend following the same approach I did, which involves purchasing a blood pressure monitoring device for approximately $25 and regularly monitoring your levels on a daily basis. You will observe a gradual decrease in these levels as you eliminate smoking from your routine. Therefore, whenever you feel tempted to smoke a cigarette, I urge you to insert your arm into the device and activate the button. After the passage of thirty seconds, the allure ceases to exist as contentment arises from the achieved outcomes.

Is it necessary for me to provide a justification?

Over the course of the past century, there has been a notable transformation in our Western culture towards immediate fulfillment. Prior to the advent of credit cards in the previous century, a substantial proportion of Americans diligently accumulated financial reserves. If one desires to acquire a remarkable Christmas gift for their children or relatives, they can avail themselves of a method known as 'layaway,' which has become exceedingly rare. Layaway refers to the process by which a customer selects a desired item, which is then reserved and stored by the retailer until it is fully paid for. You are required to make incremental payments over a span of several weeks or months in advance, and only upon completion of the final payment will the item be bestowed upon you.

It represents a complete antithesis to a credit card. By utilizing a credit card, one can acquire a desired item and subsequently settle the payment at a later date, invariably incurring additional costs that surpass the original price. In contemporary times, there is a prevalent belief that layaway is exclusively intended for individuals of limited financial means. However, it is essential to recognize that layaway, in reality, embodies an exceedingly prudent and financially conscientious method. An individual who employs the method of layaway for payment purposes exhibits a commendable characteristic that garners my utmost admiration, as it appears to be a quality that is rather uncommon in today's society. We have become accustomed to immediate fulfillment.

How many individuals declare their dietary intentions on social media simply to obtain immediate gratification? We desire the fulfillment without exerting the necessary diligence, and thus we require a genuine purpose. The satisfaction, the positive energy, and the expressions of approval we will receive for ceasing smoking will have a limited duration and are insufficient to sustain us during this undertaking.

We require an inherent form of motivation, as opposed to relying on external forms of validation.

Previous attempts to discontinue smoking have resulted in an ineffective cycle. You have yet to see success with it.

You have observed the statistics provided by the CDC. A significant portion of high school smokers have made attempts to quit or express a desire to do so, while a substantial majority of adults, approximately 70 percent, have made quit attempts within the past year. I can assure you that a significant contributing factor to the failure of numerous endeavors was the absence of a fundamental purpose.

Furthermore, we tend to commit the frequent error of engaging in a collection of habits instead of organizing our habits into a cohesive structure. A habit pile refers to the attempt to simultaneously alter multiple aspects of oneself. I do not wish for you to harbor any erroneous beliefs regarding my flawlessness. I do not possess flawless conduct, etiquette, interpersonal connections, or physical appearance. I am merely an individual who possesses more experience in smoking than yourself.

My physique is not flawless. As I endeavored to cease my smoking habit, I experienced several instances of relapse. Following each attempt at abstaining from smoking for a period, I found myself ensnared in the widely-experienced dilemma of weight gain. Although I managed to quit smoking permanently, I regrettably neglected my diet and consequently experienced a slight weight gain, while initially avoiding such consequences. Approximately one year later, owing to my immense sense of accomplishment in successfully ceasing smoking without experiencing weight gain, I proceeded to grant myself a reward in the form of weight gain. I committed a significant error of a conventional and foolish nature.

But here's the thing. subsequently, I have incorporated additional exercise routines. My body mass stably exerts a downward force, as opposed to an upward one. It is advised to refrain from attempting to incorporate multiple habits simultaneously. It would be advisable not to concurrently pursue weight loss and smoking cessation. If you adhere to a sequential methodology and approach tasks methodically, you are likely to achieve significant success. Attempting to undertake all these changes simultaneously presents an overwhelming burden, as the human body and mind do not readily adapt to such a paradigm.

In my life, I have cultivated numerous efficacious fitness practices, one of which holds a particularly personal significance. Approximately one year ago, I realized that I am faced with a significant affliction affecting my vision.

The situation deteriorated to the extent that I feared the loss of my vision, which caused me considerable distress. I earn my livelihood through my occupation as a writer. I dedicate most of my time on the computer, which led me to become deeply concerned about my ability to provide for my family in the absence of visual perception. My daughter and son are dependent on me; this responsibility weighs heavily upon me.

In the course of my investigation, I have determined that there is no issue pertaining to my vision. I am experiencing visual difficulties when using a computer. I am unable to spend twelve hours a day on a computer as I previously did during my extensive writing sessions. I'm a big writer. I've written a lot of books under many different pen names, and I've even ghostwritten over a hundred different books for clients, so losing my greatest skill terrified me.

During this particular endeavor, it dawned on me that it was imperative to secure alternative means of providing for my family in the eventuality of losing my eyesight. I proceeded to explore various techniques and technologies, eventually leading to a change in my strategy. Currently, I am the author of all of my literary works, creating them through dictation. I am continually engaged in the exploration of various methods to enhance productivity and generate content without the necessity of direct involvement with a computer.

Initially, upon commencing the task of dictation, I would position myself at the restaurant conveniently situated opposite my seaside residence. I would observe the undulating motion of the waves, review my outline, and orally transcribe. Subsequently, I transitioned and developed a novel routine. At present, I traverse a dock measuring thirty feet, oscillating above the undulating waves, continuously engaged in the act of dictation. See what I did? I have discovered a means of incorporating an additional wholesome behavior. Rather than remaining seated in front of a computer screen for twelve hours daily, I engage in three to four hours of walking, still managing to accomplish an equivalent quantity of tasks.

It required a significant investment of time to construct this procedure; yet, through an accumulation of ingrained routines, I managed to attain it. It is imperative that you refrain from the error of attempting to rectify or modify numerous habits simultaneously. Rather, focus on addressing one habit at a time to consistently improve yourself. By doing so, you can avoid feeling overwhelmed.

Ultimately, the act of ceasing smoking or initiating any habit solely due to a sense of obligation rarely proves effective. It's not enough motivation. Regrettably, acquiring unfavorable habits is quite effortless through this means, whereas acquiring advantageous ones is extremely challenging.

Recently, Steve distributed a survey to his complete audience. He inquired, "What was the primary obstacle you faced in your endeavor to cease smoking?" What has been your most significant achievement? May I inquire about the strategies or approaches you have previously employed? Our objective was to establish a profound connection with our audience, ensuring that this book resonates with the authentic experiences of all.

One observation that we made was that a number of individuals acknowledged the need to discontinue their current endeavors but lack the motivation to do so. And that's OK. You may not have reached a stage of readiness to relinquish your current circumstances, and unless you establish a compelling purposeful rationale, you are unlikely to experience the motivation to take action and ultimately cease. None of us engage in activities that do not align with our genuine desires, despite our belief that we ought to. It is universally recognized that maintaining a consistently balanced and nutritious diet is imperative. However, the reality is that the vast majority of individuals refrain from adhering to this ideal on a daily basis.

What Are The Reasons To Cease Smoking?

There must exist a compelling justification for undertaking any action. Considering the challenging nature of this procedure, individuals often find themselves contemplating the potential benefits accompanying their decision to permanently quit smoking. There exist myriad justifications for discontinuing the habit of smoking definitively. You might also find certain elements highlighted here relatable. This chapter will provide additional impetus for permanent cessation of the habit.

Ceasing the habit of tobacco smoking effectively safeguards one's well-being, presenting a highly persuasive justification for individuals to relinquish this detrimental practice to ensure their enduring physical health. In the preceding chapter, a comprehensive depiction is provided regarding the plethora of ailments that result from the habit of smoking. In addition to these, chronic cigarette smoking can instigate additional complications. Ceasing the practice of smoking considerably diminishes the likelihood of experiencing respiratory, cardiovascular, and neurological complications, among others, thereby enabling the avoidance of various potential diseases.

Cessation of smoking enhances one's well-being - In addition to mitigating the likelihood of ailments, abstaining from smoking could promptly lead to substantial improvements in one's health. An enhanced state of energy and stamina can be promptly attained owing to enhanced respiratory and cardiovascular functionality. Normalization of both heart rate and blood pressure is integral to mitigating the risk of cardiovascular diseases and ameliorating associated symptoms. Cells throughout your entire body undergo the process of regeneration, thereby diminishing the manifestations of aging.

Cessation of smoking promotes cleanliness - Maintaining cleanliness is vital for both health and ethical reasons. Indeed, the implementation of designated non-smoking areas is, to a certain extent, motivated by considerations of proper hygiene. By abstaining from tobacco use, you can avoid unpleasant consequences such as halitosis, malodorous garments, and dental discoloration, among other undesirable outcomes. Ceasing the consumption of tobacco expeditiously enhances your general hygiene.

Cessation of tobacco consumption yields notable financial benefits - The act of smoking cigarettes is an inherently deceptive habit that significantly impacts one's financial resources. When one takes into account the daily expenditures individuals allocate towards tobacco products, the cumulative expenditure over a monthly or annual period emerges as a substantial sum of money. When you quit smoking, you free up a surprisingly large amount of money for other expenses, especially for long-term heavy smokers. Therefore, refraining from indulging in the habit also yields economic advantages.

Ceasing tobacco use is widely endorsed - Worldwide initiatives promoting tobacco cessation are currently underway with great momentum. Even if you are not the type who follows trends for the sake of following them, there are certainly people who are encouraging you to drop those cigarettes down. Quitting smoking can greatly enhance your social standing through various means. Firstly, it enhances your appeal within the realm of romantic relationships. Additionally, individuals perceive those who have effectively ceased smoking as influential figures. Adopting a smoke-free lifestyle has the potential to enhance your social status significantly.

The reasons behind an individual's decision to quit smoking may vary from those of another person. Typically, it serves a noble purpose. Irrespective of the rationales you may have, it is vital to continuously bear those motivations in cognizance. Maintaining a high level of motivation will facilitate the successful transition from smoker to non-smoker. The subsequent chapters will impart the more advanced strategies required to achieve your aspiration of becoming free from tobacco use.

2

Cease the Habit of Smoking via Hypnosis: A Method for Relinquishing Smoking Utilizing Pre-recorded Hypnotic Audio

H

ypnosis

is one

Among the most widely recognized establishments for smoking cessation, studies indicate that it boasts a success rate of up to 60 percent in aiding individuals to quit their nicotine addiction. This article explores alternative methods for smoking cessation and elucidates the effectiveness of listening to therapeutic audio. Hypnosis is widely recognized as an effective method for smoking cessation, with research indicating a success rate of up to 60 percent in facilitating individuals to quit their dependency on nicotine.

This article explores alternative methods for cessation of smoking and elucidates the efficacy of consuming therapeutic audio. Smoking represents the foremost identifiable preventable cause of mortality in most developed nations and constitutes a significant contributor to the incidence of cardiac arrest, cerebral infarction, and vascular disorders. According to the National Affection Foundation, if current smoking patterns persist, it is projected that approximately 10 million fatalities per year from tobacco-related causes will be observed globally by 2025. Out of this figure, 3 million deaths are estimated to occur in developed nations, while the remaining 7 million deaths are expected in developing countries.

To provide a comparative analysis, that figure amounts to approximately three times the population of New Zealand or half the population of Australia. The plausible explanation is that consistently smoking can significantly reduce one's chance of experiencing a heart attack, making nicotine cessation the most fundamental action a smoker can take to greatly enhance their well-being. It is not incumbent upon you if you have the habit of smoking - nicotine is an inherently addictive substance of great detriment.

It exerts both physical and psychological influence on you. There are those who assert that abandoning the habit of smoking is more challenging than abstaining from heroin. A study conducted by New Scientist Magazine in 1992 reported that hypnotic therapy, administered in a single session, yielded a success rate of up to 60 percent in assisting individuals in smoking cessation.

Acupuncture constituted an additional 24 percent, trailed by nicotine replacement therapy at 10 percent, and pure cessation without any external aids, commonly referred to as 'cold turkey', at 6 percent. According to a study conducted by the American Journal of Preventive Medicine, it has been found that fewer than seven percent of individuals who attempt to quit smoking without assistance are successful in achieving long-term abstinence from nicotine after a year. An overwhelming 93 percent fail in their endeavors due to their partial commitment, as they only relied on their familiarized mindset.

The concept behind this agency is that although a smoker may express the desire to quit, it is merely a reflection of their conscious thought process. If the subconscious mind has ingrained the belief that 'I can never give up smoking because I've attempted to do so in the past and found it exceedingly challenging,' it will supersede any conscious thoughts suggesting otherwise. Hypnotism possesses the capacity to encourage and persuade your subconscious mind to adopt a new belief that you are completely devoid of the habit of smoking, whilst simultaneously guiding you towards manifesting and maintaining a non-smoking lifestyle.

Through the use of anesthetic abstraction, it can be affirmed that you possess a strong aversion to the taste, scent, and visual presentation associated with cigarettes. You require both familiar and concealed determination to overcome the nicotine addiction, and employing therapeutic methods can enhance your resolve and bolster your ability to maintain this determination. When you are under the influence of an analgesic, it is possible for you to experience anxiety about embracing new challenges and altering your customary response to situations where you habitually resort to smoking.

Analgesic can be employed to discern the fundamental requirements that a smoker endeavors to fulfill for an individual, such as justifying taking a respite or providing as a form of gratification. It can be utilized to enhance an individual's determination to cease, bolster their resolve to make healthier lifestyle choices, alleviate feelings of anxiety, reduce cravings, or enable them to be less influenced when in the presence of others who smoke. Hypnotism should not be considered a miraculous solution, as numerous specialists strongly advise that it should only serve as one element among many tools – including dietary adjustments, physical activity, and cultivating a more positive mindset – that individuals desiring to quit smoking should employ.

Quit Day

Within the framework of all tobacco cessation approaches, a designated cessation date is supplied, which signifies the definitive cessation of smoking. This particular day is frequently regarded with trepidation and apprehension, akin to a day of "collective evaluation" wherein the smoker must undergo a rigorous test, serving as a means of self-purification.

Nomore wrong. The cessation day should be regarded with the apprehension akin to that experienced on the final day of the academic year or the concluding day of work prior to holidays. The day on which you undergo a transformation, rather than the day you encounter an examination. For the better.

However, how can we effectively handle the challenges of the present day?

In preparation for the quit day, it is highly recommended to dispose of lighters, cigarette packages, ashtrays, and any other items that may trigger reminders of smoking. This should be done on the day prior to abstaining from cigarettes. In addition, it is advisable to remove any items that carry the scent of smoke, as they may serve as triggers for the desire to smoke. This includes washing the vehicle, taking a refreshing shower, and ensuring that clean clothing is prepared for the following day, encompassing everything from undergarments to outerwear. I kindly request that my relatives, friends, and colleagues be informed that as of tomorrow, I am committed to ceasing my smoking habit and kindly ask that they refrain from offering me any cigarettes.

What activities can be undertaken on the day of departure?

The initial guideline pertains to the alteration of habits. Some suggestions:1. If you have been provided with a prescription for medications, ensure that you adhere to the recommended dosage and administration instructions. Extensive research has been conducted in preparation for this occasion, therefore refrain from amplifying it solely for the purpose of seeking reinforcement. If you opt to have your breakfast at home in the morning, consider visiting a bar instead (and vice versa)3. Consider storing sugar-free chewing gum and/or candy in your pocket for convenient use throughout the day. 1. Remember to carry a writing instrument, a keychain, a cocoa butter or lipstick, or any similar compact item that can be utilized for diversion during intervals or when your hands are unoccupied. 2. Consider rescheduling the designated "coffee break" for a more convenient time or alternatively, abstain from consuming coffee altogether. 3. Make alternative arrangements for the allocated period of relaxation or cessation, preferably without incorporating the consumption of caffeinated beverages. Please consider bringing a bottle of water to be consumed immediately after the coffee, as a replacement for the cigarette, if abstaining from smoking becomes challenging for you. Please bear in mind: It is important to resist the impulse to engage in smoking. It has a duration of several minutes, therefore employ the method involving the water bottle whenever you experience the inclination to. It works!7. If you consistently frequent the same dining establishment, you may consider either returning home or choosing to dine within the confines of your office, or alternatively, exploring alternative locations. In the presence of others, kindly inform everyone about your decision to quit smoking, ensuring they are aware not to offer you cigarettes or smoke in proximity to you.

Avoid consciously attempting to suppress thoughts of cigarettes, as this may inadvertently cause them to persistently occupy your thoughts throughout the day. However, should the suggestion weigh heavily on your mind and become excessively bothersome, take action by rising from your seat and engaging in a task or activity. Engage in any activity, be it going for a stroll, disposing of the rubbish, recalibrating the decoder, irrespective of the task at hand, as long as you maintain physical involvement.

One final piece of advice: refrain from imbuing your quit day with an excessive number of connotations. This does not mark the commencement of a fresh chapter in life, as the world at large (including your personal circumstances) will not inherently grow more exquisite: professional responsibilities will continue to induce stress, mortgage payments will persist at their current level, your neighbor will perpetually subject you to the irksome blare of their television, and your favored sports team will, regrettably, face defeat once more in the derby encounter.

You will come to realize that you can manage all of these challenges even in the absence of cigarettes.

Throughout the recovery process, it is imperative to bear in mind the following advantages of quitting smoking: "Within a span of 20 minutes, both blood pressure and heart rate regain their usual levels." "Following a lapse of 24 hours, the respiratory system initiates a natural process of eliminating mucus and residues caused by smoking, leading to an improvement in bad breath." Enhance taste and olfactory perception" Within a span of three days, you will experience an improvement in respiratory function and the rejuvenation of energy. Between two to twelve weeks, there will be a noticeable enhancement in blood circulation. After three to nine months, the progress in respiratory performance becomes more pronounced. Corticgations and respiratory noises wane or desist. After the course of one calendar year, the cardiovascular peril diminishes by half in comparison to the cohort that persists in tobacco consumption. The incidence of lung cancer has significantly reduced by 50% in many cases after a duration of 10 years, resulting in a risk comparable to that of individuals who have never smoked or, alternatively, a 50% reduction (depending on various factors such as daily cigarette consumption, duration of smoking, and coexisting medical conditions). Furthermore, after a span of 15 years, the risk of cardiovascular diseases, such as heart attacks, reaches a level equivalent to that of non-smokers. The mortality rate, encompassing all possible causes, nearly matches that of individuals who have never engaged in smoking.

Smoking has detrimental effects on your physical health.

The impacts of smoking start right away. After the inhalation of the initial inhalation of smoke, it merely takes a brief span of 10 seconds for the nicotine medication to reach the brain, as described by experts at the Cancer Research UK. In its role as a stimulant, it elicits an increase in both heart rate and blood pressure, proving to be equally addictive as other substances such as heroin or cocaine. The protracted effects, however, appear to be quite compelling... .

• Pulmonary system: Are you able to engage in respiration? A significant majority of individuals do so, yet smoking has the potential to exacerbate the issue. It inflicts damage upon the entire respiratory system, including the trachea, the bronchi branching out from the trachea, and the minute air sacs within the lungs, known as alveoli. Typically, chronic cigarette smoking leads to the development of chronic obstructive pulmonary disease (COPD). This terminology describes a compilation of ailments comprising bronchitis (which causes damage to the bronchi) and emphysema (which causes damage to the air sacs). Should you happen to suffer from asthma, which falls under the category of chronic obstructive pulmonary disease, it is highly probable that smoking will worsen its symptoms. Furthermore, it is evident that smoking frequently leads directly to the occurrence of pulmonary deterioration.

While endeavoring to assist his mother in a general sense concerning his decision to engage in smoking, a young individual further remarked, "Furthermore, it is worth noting that upon cessation, your respiratory organs will undergo a restorative process."

Indeed, a consensus among experts in this field suggests that the cilia within your respiratory system commence their regenerative process once smoking is discontinued, thereby reducing the risk of developing lung cancer by half after a decade.

That is indeed promising news for individuals who have quit smoking. Regardless, it is not a logically valid rationale to possess a favorable perspective towards initiating smoking. According to experts from Harvard Medical School, even after a decade, the associated risks remain higher compared to if one had never smoked at all. The risk you face may eventually become comparable to that of a non-smoker if you choose to quit at a young age. In view of all factors taken into account, why even commence in any manner? Why endure the struggle of becoming reliant and failing to ascertain the determination to cease?

•Cardiovascular health: Smoking significantly increases the likelihood of developing heart disease and experiencing a stroke. As the thickness of your blood vessels increases and their size diminishes, your heart will exert greater effort and consequently, your blood pressure will rise. Irrespective of the frequency of smoking being limited to less than five cigarettes per day, individuals may begin to exhibit early symptoms of cardiovascular disease, as stated by the Centers for Disease Control and Prevention (CDC).

• Increased damage to organs: In addition to affecting the heart and lungs, the Centers for Disease Control and Prevention (CDC) acknowledges that smoking adversely affects nearly every organ in the body and can potentially lead to the development of various types of cancer in different areas, such as...

Bladder

Blood

Cervix

Large intestine, specifically the colon and rectum

Esophagus

Renal and ureteral

Larynx

Liver

Pharynx, lingual apparatus, palatine glands

Pancreas

Stomach

• Skeletal System: The act of smoking has a deleterious effect on the structural integrity of your bones, particularly as you age, thereby elevating the likelihood of developing fractures and fractures.

• Eyes: If you are concerned about preserving your vision as you age, smoking would not be optimal. Engaging in smoking will elevate your risk for both the development of cataracts and age-related macular degeneration.

- Teeth and gums: Undoubtedly, any form of tobacco usage will directly impact your dental well-being. WebMD documents a plethora of dental conditions resulting from smoking, including periodontal disease, dental discoloration, jawbone depletion, and, naturally, oral carcinoma.

- Maternity: The act of smoking during pregnancy is detrimental to both the mother and the developing baby. The Centers for Disease Control and Prevention (CDC) provides clarification that the risk of an ectopic pregnancy will increase, concomitantly elevating the risk of experiencing a stillbirth. Your infant is likely to have a below-average birth weight and this will increase the likelihood of him experiencing Sudden Infant Death Syndrome.

Furthermore, when it comes to the topic of infants, I would like to address the male perspective. If you aspire to become a father, it is advisable for you to refrain from tobacco consumption, as smoking has been shown to negatively impact your reproductive abilities.

• Additional conditions and illnesses: Certainly, there is something else. Smoking is a contributing factor to the development of both type 2 diabetes and rheumatoid arthritis. It also induces irritation throughout the body and weakens the immune function, thereby leading to numerous diseases. Additionally, while occasional smoking may aid in weight management, there seems to be an apparent correlation between intensive smoking and weight gain. (Furthermore, would you not agree that there are more effective methods for achieving weight loss?)

•Demise: It is not a topic that is generally well-received. However, if you do intend to smoke, it is highly advisable to carefully deliberate upon it. Tobacco use contributes to a staggering 90% of cellular deterioration leading to lung-related fatalities, as well as being responsible for 80% of deaths resulting from Chronic Obstructive Pulmonary

Disease (COPD). It is possible that the CDC findings did not surprise you; however, it is noteworthy to mention that cigarette smoking significantly increases the likelihood of mortality from various causes. According to the National Center for Biotechnology Information, between 33% and 50% of individuals who are long-term smokers pass away due to their addiction.

Should the absence of substantial physical damage fail to be a compelling factor, it would be prudent to consider several alternative implications of smoking that may adversely affect one's life.

We are solely addressing a behavioral pattern.

I would like to emphasize a key point, and I would greatly appreciate your focused attention. Should you fail to recall any other points of our discussion, please retain this particular message in your memory. Our sole objective here is to cease a recurring behavior. Smoking is a mere behavioral pattern. That concludes the matter, in a straightforward manner. Society endeavors to elevate it to a higher degree. It is no disparate from procrastination, excessive eating, nail-chewing, or any other detrimental habit we have acquired throughout our journey. Nonetheless, our routines, be they beneficial or detrimental, often serve as narratives that adhere to a straightforward principle of cause and effect.

Our smoking constitutes a mere habit that we shall overcome collectively, expeditiously and effortlessly. I have successfully accomplished the task, and rest assured, you too shall achieve the same outcome by diligently adhering to the prescribed methodology. If fully embraced, the process is unequivocally infallible. It consistently displays a success rate of 100%, without any instances of deviation.

However, it should be noted that any action carried out consistently over a prolonged duration will inevitably develop into a habit, making this principle universally applicable. It is not inherently unfavorable, but rather a neutral matter. When we attain mastery over our habits, they grant us unparalleled liberty; however, should we succumb to the influence of our habits, they shall render us captive. The term addiction can be broadly defined as "being subjected to the control of a habitual behavior." Does it appear to be comprehensible? It is simply a behavioral pattern that I have developed. Regrettably, I must reiterate this point in order to underscore its importance. It is of utmost significance to comprehend this, as it holds paramount importance for our collective success. The inherent marvel of the complete arrangement, this endeavor we refer to as life, lies in our ability to reclaim command. It is imperative that we reclaim control over our lives. Our negative tendencies wield power over us solely if we permit them. Cigarettes exert control over our lives solely to the extent that we permit them to do so. It is merely a customary practice.

There is a glimmer of hope on the horizon, and the path to success is considerably briefer than anticipated. You are embarking on a journey that will have a profound and permanent impact on your life. You will no longer rely on cigarettes for your nicotine cravings. Never again will you fail to live up to the expectations of those in your vicinity. Henceforth, you shall no longer experience feelings of inadequacy, weakness, lack of control, dependency, helplessness, or depression. No more smoking. Kindly articulate the phrase,

"Smoking is prohibited from this point forward." Those times have concluded, my companion, and it commences precisely in this present moment.

It all begins with a choice. "The term 'Decision' is formally defined as follows:

The process of arriving at a decision or resolving an inquiry, ascertaining, as of a matter or uncertainty.

The process or necessity of reaching a decision

An outcome that has been determined; a definitive conclusion.

The attribute of being resolute; steadfastness.

A genuine decision eliminates all alternative options. Expressing a desire to cease smoking is merely a proposition. Making the decision to quit smoking is a decisive resolution that leaves no room for alternative choices. Indeed, it is evident that individuals possess the capability to voluntarily withdraw from any commitment or activity without restriction. It all commences with a crucial determination. This present moment presents us with a novel chance for growth and progress, rendering past experiences inconsequential. You have evidently arrived at the determination to cease smoking, as evidenced by your decision to peruse this publication. You would refrain from devoting your time to perusing it. Deciding to quit smoking, or making any affirmative decision for that matter, possesses a spirit of liberation. It provides liberation! Once an individual commits wholeheartedly, all alternative possibilities are effectively eradicated. Attaining the ultimate state of freedom lies in the choice to quit smoking, after which the path becomes remarkably smooth.

Our main emphasis will be directed towards the resolution rather than the issue at hand. This book is presented in a succinct, concise, and straightforward manner. Our objective is to achieve optimal outcomes within the most expedient timeframe. In other terms, our time will not be expended. I do not possess any interest in delving into your personal history, intimate connections, deep-seated fears, or any other topic, for that matter. The issue at hand is apparent; we desire to cease smoking. That's why we're here. We made a spontaneous decision to start smoking that initial cigarette, and we retain the power to make an immediate decision to discontinue the habit. There exists no distinction; our perception merely suggests its existence. We merely acknowledge the anticipated complexity due to our conditioned beliefs.

We will be harnessing our most valuable asset, our intellect. The human brain possesses unparalleled computational capabilities and, when harnessed effectively, can function as an asset rather than a liability. I will now elucidate the process of reprogramming the aforementioned computer, as well as impart the knowledge on how to effectively reprogram one's own cognitive faculties. Permanently eradicating the inclination to smoke is analogous to activating a mental switch, whereby we will consciously initiate this transformative process. This shall be the course of action: we shall effectively retrain our minds, achieving this endeavor with an unsurpassed level of ease that surpasses any previous notion of possibility.

Nevertheless, a choice remains futile unless it is accompanied by resolute and expeditious implementation. Without implementation, it remains merely a conceptualization. Absence of action renders it mere fanciful contemplation. The course of action you are about to pursue aligns with the established procedures explicated in this publication. The sole requirement I seek from you pertains to your inclination towards ceasing the habit of smoking, coupled with your unwavering dedication to adhere meticulously to the prescribed procedure. I am committed to fulfilling my responsibilities and my utmost aspiration is for your success to be achieved. I am fully dedicated to ensuring your success.

If you are dissatisfied with the current state of your life stemming from smoking and seek improvement, then you possess the aspiration. If you are willing to continue reading and adhere to the process as detailed, you have demonstrated your dedication. Both a strong desire and unwavering commitment are essential ingredients that will ensure your success as we progress.

You should now possess absolute clarity regarding your desired objective, which is to permanently cease your smoking habit. Not merely for a short duration of time, be it a day, week, month, or year, but for an indeterminate and enduring period. The approach delineated in this literary work presents a lasting remedy tailored for individuals who have resolved to discontinue their smoking habits promptly. Should one merely entertain the notion of quitting, it becomes imperative to reassess and reflect upon their commitment. However, provided that you are genuinely prepared, having made a sincere resolution and a truthful commitment, we are prepared to proceed forward.

Prior to proceeding, allocate a brief period to relish the lucidity and tranquility of mind that arises from arriving at a genuine determination. It's ultimate freedom. Please pause to envision the future state of your life, liberated from the enslavement of nicotine for eternity.

As previously indicated, a decision holds solely as an idea unless promptly accompanied by subsequent action. Please bear in mind that the process consistently yields positive results. The same strategy that proves effective for one individual will likely yield positive outcomes for others as well. Enacting the Decision to cease smoking, we should promptly proceed towards Chapter 2 through actionable steps.

Nicotine Replacement Therapy (Nrt) As A Means Of Providing Physical Assistance In Smoking Cessation

Nicotine dependence exerts a dual impact on your physiological and psychological well-being. To successfully combat this addiction, a comprehensive approach encompassing psychological assistance, modification of one's lifestyle, and appropriate medication is necessary. In the following chapter, we will be examining the physiological aspects encompassing smoking cessation.

NRT, otherwise known as Nicotine Replacement Therapy

As an habitual tobacco consumer, one develops a rapid reliance on the nicotine contained within the cigarettes. Nicotine replacement therapy, or NRT, administers a controlled dosage of nicotine to your system, devoid of the accompanying harmful additives found in tobacco. One can employ inhalers, gums, sprays, patches, or lozenges to regulate their nicotine craving and redirect their attention towards the psychological aspects of smoking cessation.

How NRT works

As an individual who frequently engages in smoking, you possess first-hand knowledge regarding the arduousness of abstaining from smoking, even for a brief period. Upon embarking on the cessation journey, individuals who smoke immediately experience potent withdrawal symptoms as a result of nicotine dependency. Between seventy and ninety percent of individuals who engage in smoking experience difficulty in ceasing this habit due to this sole factor.

NRT gradually mitigates these symptoms and assists the patient in managing their nicotine cravings. The United States Food and Drug Administration, commonly known as the FDA, has granted approval to five types of nicotine replacement therapy.

Nicotine patches deliver a controlled dosage of nicotine transdermally. You have the option to utilize a patch with a duration of sixteen hours or continuous coverage. Select the patches that most appropriately align with your needs and preferences. It is imperative that you initiate the treatment with a patch that has its maximum potency and adhere to its usage for a period of one month. In the event of a successful outcome, proceed to a less robust segment in the upcoming month.

A prescription will be required for the usage of nicotine nasal sprays, unlike patches. Nasal sprays exhibit a expedited response as compared to patches due to the direct absorption of nicotine through the nasal passage, which promptly regulates nicotine cravings. Nasal sprays are highly user-friendly, thereby garnering favor among smokers due to their efficacy in providing prompt alleviation. It is advised to refrain from exceeding a duration of six months when using nasal sprays, as prolonged usage can engender dependence and give rise to additional complications.

Nicotine inhalers consist of a cartridge filled with nicotine. They administer nicotine orally and facilitate rapid absorption into the bloodstream. It is recommended to utilize a daily quantity of four to 20 cartridges over the span of six months.

Nicotine gum: The utilization of nicotine gum is highly convenient. Continue chewing nicotine gum until a distinct peppery sensation is perceived in the oral cavity. Cease masticating and retain the chewing gum within your oral cavity. Resume mastication once the pungent flavor subsides. Continue this sequence for a duration of 20 to 30 minutes. Abstain from consuming any food or beverage directly prior to or directly subsequent to masticating the gum.

Non-prescription access is granted for nicotine lozenges, enabling their utilization without the need for a prescription. For optimal results, it is recommended to utilize lozenges consistently over a duration of three months. Gently and gradually dissolve the lozenge in your mouth, refraining from biting, chewing, or ingesting it. Do refrain from ingesting any substance within a quarter of an hour prior to or subsequent to the ingestion of nicotine lozenges.

Choose your NRT

While all NRTs possess identical characteristics, certain options may be better suited to your needs. Certain varieties may not effectively cater to your specific requirements. "It is imperative to take into account several factors prior to choosing your nicotine replacement therapy:

If expedient outcomes are of importance to you, then the nasal spray is a suitable option.

Inhalers enable individuals to replicate the act of smoking cigarettes and exert control over their physiological cravings.

The act of chewing gum or utilizing inhalers or lozenges serves to effectively divert one's attention and effectively address nicotine cravings.

If you do not possess any skin sensitivities or allergies, it is recommended to utilize nicotine patches.

A prescription is necessary for the acquisition of inhalers and nasal sprays.

In the situation where an individual is afflicted with diabetes, it is advised to employ sugar-free lozenges and nicotine gums.

Therapeutic Herbal Remedies For Smoking Cessation

In addition to obtaining over-the-counter medications, there exist herbal supplements that facilitate the cessation of smoking via natural means. This approach is considerably safer and, not to mention, more cost-effective compared to acquiring pharmaceuticals prescribed by your healthcare provider. These herbal supplements may occasionally be sourced from one's immediate surroundings, such as the garden or the culinary area of one's residence.

Lobelia

Alternatively known as lobelia inflata, this plant consists of lobeline, a compound that has the potential to mitigate the desire for nicotine. It is important to highlight that this functions similarly to nicotine, as has been indicated by several studies conducted in Maryland. This lobeline exhibits non-addictive properties and is employed as a therapeutic intervention for nicotine withdrawal symptoms. Nevertheless, this particular substance has not obtained the approval of the Federal Drug Administration (FDA) in its designation as an herbal remedy for smoking cessation. This lack of approval is due to its significant similarity to nicotine, as it shares similar effects such as bronchiole dilation, perspiration, emesis, diarrhea, queasiness, disorientation, seizures, cognitive impairment, and in severe cases, fatality. If you desire to experience the potential benefits of this particular herb, it is imperative that you exclusively employ it under the guidance and oversight of a licensed healthcare professional. It is imperative to seek guidance from individuals possessing sufficient expertise, as prioritizing caution over regret is of utmost importance in the final analysis.

Oat Straw

The oat straw, scientifically known as Avina sativa, is widely regarded as one of the most extensively documented herbal remedies for aiding individuals in their endeavor to quit smoking through natural means. This information has been sourced from the Peace Health Organization. This oat straw is comprised of avenine glycosides that have the effect of stimulating the central nervous system and simultaneously enhancing our circulatory function. The augmentation of blood circulation within an individual's system can serve to alleviate the withdrawal symptoms associated with the act of smoking.

St. John's Wort

Commonly known as hypericum perforatum, St. John's wort is renowned for its efficacy in treating conditions commonly referred to as nervous disorders. This herb possesses the ability to address skin concerns, alleviate infections, mitigate the effects of hemorrhoids, and potentially alleviate symptoms of depression, as it is reputed for its mood-improving properties. This is also the rationale behind the widespread prescription of St. John's wort, among other herbal remedies, to individuals seeking assistance in smoking cessation. Nevertheless, it is not recommended for women who are currently pregnant or breastfeeding to utilize this product. Once again, it is imperative to seek the advice of a healthcare professional before considering the utilization of such herbal supplements.

Valerian

Valerian, scientifically referred to as Valeriana offcinalis, is a herbal remedy employed for smoking cessation purposes. It functions effectively as a sedative when ingested. A naturally occurring sedative proves highly efficacious in inducing a profound state of tranquility during the process of nicotine withdrawal. For enhanced efficacy, the combination of lemon balm and St. John's Wort with it would yield an antidepressant-like effect. Moreover, it is imperative that this be incorporated into one's daily routine, but only after consulting with a qualified expert.

Ginseng and Others

I would highly recommend considering ginseng as another herbal remedy worth exploring. Ginseng possesses the potential to mitigate the inclination towards smoking by reducing stress levels, as it is widely acknowledged that stress serves as a catalyst for the desire to smoke. Additional herbal supplements that can be considered are those derived from peppermint and cinnamon bark.

Methods to Quit Smoking

There exist numerous approaches to cease the habit of smoking. Certain approaches are grounded in scientific principles and rely heavily on concrete outcomes, whereas other approaches, although lacking scientific validity, have proven effective for certain individuals. In the forthcoming chapter, we will explore the most validated scientific methodologies that can be employed for smoking cessation. Once more, ultimately, it pertains to the individual's determination. It is imperative that you bear in mind this aspect prior to embarking upon the lifelong journey of smoking cessation.

In this chapter, we shall explore a selection of renowned and beneficial approaches to smoking cessation. Please bear in mind that not every approach may be compatible with your preferred lifestyle. You must demonstrate astuteness in order to select the optimal option that suits your needs precisely. If all proceeds smoothly, it can be assured that you will imminently cease your smoking habit.

The Journal Approach

One possible alternative in a formal tone could be: "The initial approach entails the establishment of a journal." While this notion may initially provoke a sense of amusement or appear trivial in nature, it will undeniably prove exceedingly beneficial in the broader context of smoking cessation and subsequent recovery phases. This journal does not necessitate formality since it will remain exclusively between you and no one else. It is imperative that it addresses a few inquiries. One could designate their journal as the "Craving Chronicle," a repository for documenting various aspects of cravings, including the timing of cigarette cravings, the underlying causes, potential triggers, emotional states experienced during cravings, and similar related points. This particular approach is widely renowned as one of the most acclaimed techniques for cessation of smoking. This approach is self-guided, wherein you assume full responsibility for assisting yourself throughout the entirety of the process. This process may span several weeks, or even months; however, it is undoubtedly a highly effective and enduring approach.

Question Method

Another well-known technique is referred to as the widely recognized interrogative approach. This may likely be the most challenging approach among all. There is no need for any action beyond engaging your mental faculties when utilizing this approach. This approach is contingent upon a crucial inquiry that you will pose to yourself whilst occupying a position before a reflective surface. The inquiry at hand is, "What is the reason behind my smoking?" What is the underlying cause?" Research indicates that friends exert significant influence when it comes to smoking behavior, thereby suggesting that one possible explanation for your smoking habits could be the direct influence of your friends. Furthermore, it is permissible for you to engage in smoking as it serves as a means to alleviate the distress brought about by undesirable encounters. You are also permitted to smoke for recreational purposes. Try to dig deep. It appears evident that you currently engage in smoking due to personal satisfaction, although it is evident that this was not your original motivation. Scarcely anyone initiates smoking for the purpose of deriving pleasure from it. Pleasure is always derived from regular practice. You must endeavor to identify the underlying causation that prompted the initiation of your smoking habit. If one is able to identify the underlying cause, they can proceed to implement appropriate measures to address it. For instance, should you come to the realization that acquaintances were the impetus behind your initiation into smoking, it is imperative to disassociate yourself from those acquaintances. If they are your close acquaintances, it would be beneficial to communicate to them your sincere desire to abstain from smoking and your need for their assistance in order to successfully accomplish this objective. If they do not constitute your inner circle, it would be advisable to refrain from any contact with them for a minimum duration of two months. All research studies have consistently demonstrated that successfully abstaining from smoking for a duration of two months serves as a pivotal milestone, enabling individuals to effectively cease smoking for the entirety of their lives.

Avoid Triggers

Considering that you have previously engaged with a journal in the second chapter of this book, you possess an understanding of your specific triggers and the factors that can heighten the inclination to smoke. It is essential that you exercise control over those triggers at this juncture. Does the act of smoking primarily result from attending social gatherings, or is it more closely influenced by prolonged exposure to television? Identify the catalyst and devise an alternative strategy for each circumstance. It is important to bear in mind that abstaining from social gatherings and indulging in recreational activities is not a viable solution, as doing so may engender feelings of melancholy and eventually lead to a relapse into smoking. It is imperative to strike a harmonious equilibrium whereby both the physical and mental aspects of oneself find contentment in the resolution. I would like to offer a small recommendation that will certainly be beneficial. For instance, if you happen to be in the habit of smoking whenever engaged in telephone conversations, it would be advisable to provision each of your telephones with a pen and paper. Henceforth, whenever you receive a telephone call, endeavor to engage yourself with the use of a pen and paper. This will be greatly beneficial. This is the approach through which one can proactively circumvent the triggering factors.

Why Don't You Delay?

Postponing is a timid strategy of relinquishing the habit of smoking, yet undeniably an efficacious one. If you have a feeling that you will crave for smoking in a few minutes then tell yourself that you can wait ten more minutes before you start smoking, and then take another ten minutes for your body. Endeavor to promote engagement in alternate activities during this interim period. Your physique also possesses an inherent understanding that smoking is an unfavorable habit, and by prolonging the period of abstention, the compulsion to smoke shall gradually dissipate.

Mastication is an Excellent Method

An extensively renowned method for curbing the craving to smoke involves incessantly chewing on an object. The item in question may manifest as a chewing gum, as is commonly the case, or alternatively as chocolate or unflavored rubber gums. The decision regarding which one you will choose to chew lies solely in your hands. When engaged in a persistent act of chewing, the human body will cease its mental preoccupation with tobacco, thereby gradually diminishing the mind's inclination or desire for it. This entails a process of considerable duration. The cessation of smoking using this method typically requires approximately two months. Please be advised that smoking is strictly prohibited at all times during this designated period. If you engage in the act of smoking even once, your capacity to commence this endeavor anew will unequivocally be compromised. It is perpetually an instance of seizing the present or losing the opportunity indefinitely.

Be cautious of the potential pitfalls of succumbing to the 'one trap'.

If you are acquainted with individuals who have effectively ceased smoking in the past, and if you inquire about the primary hindrance they encountered, you will gain insight into the phenomenon referred to as the one trap syndrome. It possesses an inherent simplicity coupled with a formidable level of complexity to manage. The human psyche is a fascinating phenomenon that often tempts one to indulge in a final cigarette prior to permanently forsaking the habit. Exercise caution and avoid succumbing to this single pitfall. If you consume a drink before departing, it is highly likely that you will continue to consume subsequent drinks. Upon cessation of smoking, one abandons the habit permanently, thereby making an irrevocable commitment to refrain from it altogether. No circumstance will have the power to alter that determination. Maintain this mindset and you will undoubtedly have the ability to cease smoking.

Be Active

While exercise may not directly contribute to smoking cessation, it does have an indirect impact that can be beneficial. Researchers have established that engaging in a regular regimen of physical activity for a duration of thirty minutes on a daily basis can effectively assist in combating the detrimental effects of tobacco consumption. The significance of tobacco may not be readily apparent if one engages in a daily exercise regimen of at least thirty minutes. If you possess a sufficient amount of time at your disposal, I recommend considering the option of enrolling in a fitness facility or engaging in a daily outdoor running routine. If you find yourself lacking sufficient time for that activity, alternatively, you may engage in exercises such as pushups, pull-ups, walking, crunches, and other fundamental exercises within the confines of your own residence.

Let's Fight Together

If one engages in online exploration, one may come across numerous virtual platforms and communities that can be utilized as channels for seeking direct assistance. You will encounter numerous individuals who are grappling with circumstances similar to yours, all dedicated to a shared objective. There exists a proverb which proclaims that it is prudent to have two individuals aboard a vessel if one desires to prematurely reach the designated boundary. In these public discourse platforms and communities, you will discover not merely a pair of individuals, but rather a multitude of individuals united in their shared commitment to mutual support and assistance. Assistance derived from personal experience is invariably superior to the theoretical knowledge regarding strategies for abstaining from smoking. Engage in a conversation with them for a minimum of ten minutes daily. If you take this action, you will experience an immediate enhancement in your motivation.

Remind Yourself the Benefits

Within the depths of your consciousness, you are well aware that the act of smoking poses detrimental consequences to the human physique. Regardless of your actions, it is imperative that you bear this in mind. Furthermore, consistently strive to reinforce in your mind the positive outcomes that would result from successfully abstaining from smoking. An alternative suggestion would be to compose a comprehensive list on a large sheet of paper detailing the various positive outcomes that can be anticipated upon cessation of smoking. Once you have transcribed all the information onto the paper, affix it to a prominent location in order to draw attention to it. Your subconscious faculties will attend to all matters.

There are several notable advantages that you can obtain by abstaining from smoking. Presented below are a selection of examples:

You will no longer experience the physical discomfort that was associated with your previous smoking habit.

You are likely to experience fewer ailments if you refrain from smoking.

Would you consider yourself to be overweight? Cease smoking and observe the notable distinction.

Would you like to cultivate swiftness and vigor in order to garner favor with others? Cease the act of smoking and experience the discernible disparities.

Would you be interested in improving the condition of your cardiovascular system? Stop Smoking

Do you wish for individuals in your proximity to perish due to your actions? If such is not the case, then cease the act of smoking.

Could you please share your personal inclination towards the act of inhabiting? Smoking has been proven to have lethal consequences within a relatively short span of a few years. Stop now.

www.ingramcontent.com/pod-product-compliance
Lightning Source LLC
Chambersburg PA
CBHW050251120526
44590CB00016B/2310